MUSEUM OF LONDON

EIGHTEENTH
CENTURY
LONDON

Nichola Johnson

London: HMSO

CREDITS

Copyright in the illustrations rests with the Museum of London with the following exceptions:

Charlotte Fitzroy by Lely (p 8), *York City Art Gallery*; Ignatius Sancho by Gainsborough (p 9), *National Gallery of Canada, Ottawa*; 19th-century interior of Bevis Marks Synagogue (p 9), *The Jewish Museum*; bust of Wesley (p 15), *Wesley's Chapel*; title page to 'Authentic Narrative...' (p 27), *Metropolitan Police Museum*; Marriage à la Mode by Hogarth (p 34), *The Trustees, National Gallery, London*; Sale of a Wife in Smithfield Market (p 37), *Guildhall Library*.

Photographs: Barrington Gray, Torla Evans, John Chase, John Edwards.

Cartography: Sally Fentiman.

I should like to thank friends and colleagues, both at the Museum of London and at other institutions, for their generous help in the preparation and production of this book.

(*Inside front cover*) Southwark Fair, engraving by William Hogarth, 1733.
(*Title page*) A reconstruction of a corridor in Newgate Gaol, with original doors.

© Copyright of the Board of Governors of the Museum of London 1991
First published 1991

ISBN 0 11 290448 3

British Library Cataloguing in Publication Data
A CIP catalogue record for this book is available from the British Library

CONTENTS

Discovering Eighteenth-Century London

To most people the 18th century is synonymous with elegance, refinement and 'good taste' in everything from architecture and furnishings to music and literature. But this is only one side of the story. A close look at the fascinating and sometimes horrifying world in which the majority of 18th-century Londoners lived reveals how unbalanced this popular picture of the period really is.

London was a city of dramatic contrasts, between rich and poor, new money and old, continuity and rapid change. While in some respects the 18th-century city still reflected its medieval past, in others it was moving rapidly towards its present position as a centre for services, and for the conspicuous consumption of everything from 'fast food' to opera. Though much of the old City was

William Marlow's painting of 1762 shows the north end of old London Bridge from Fresh Wharf, and gives some idea of the essentially medieval huddle of buildings in the City.

still a maze of courts and alleyways even at the end of the century, a walk along the Strand towards the West End would have taken us past elegant riverside palaces and pockets of extreme poverty to the spacious new developments to the east of Hyde Park, and to the old Oxford road, already a great shopping centre. Here, Londoners and foreigners window-shopped, stole and bought, very much as they do today.

It is not only our shopping habits which link us to 18th-century London. Many of the institutions and practices which we take for granted today developed during this time, some of them from roots established in the late 17th century. The 1700s saw the consolidation of a national banking system, with a regulated currency, based on the Bank of England's present site in Threadneedle Street. Some foremost banks and insurance, stock and commodity broking firms in the City began life in the coffee houses of London over 200 years ago. The capital's great teaching hospitals were established as a result of growing philanthropic concern, and new public dispensaries were the forerunners of the clinics and general practices upon which most modern Londoners still rely.

It is to the 18th century, too, that we owe the first really methodical system of street-naming and numbering: the relative vagueness of an address – 'by the sign of the Golden Cockerel at the corner of Cheapside opposite the entrance to Bow Lane' – may sound rather romantic now, but it was a useless way of identifying the thousands of new premises springing up as a result of London's rapid expansion! Our existing sewage, paving and street-lighting systems also have their origins in Acts of Parliament passed at this time.

Such associations of past and present can, of course, be applied to almost any period of London's history. The layout of parts of the Roman city can be traced in today's street pattern; and from street names, the areas in which many of the city's medieval trading and commercial activities were concentrated can be deduced. But comparatively little of pre-18th-century London remains above ground, whereas physical and documentary evidence of the city since 1700 is much richer.

In spite of two wars, and development and redevelopment over two centuries, there is still a great deal to be seen of the capital as it then was. Some of the places you can visit are listed at the end of this booklet. Buildings, though, tell only a small part of the story. To find out about the lives people led in and among those buildings, and in the parts of the 18th-century city which are now lost, we need to look at a great deal more than bricks and stone. We must look at the objects that people left behind them, read the words in which they recorded their impressions, experiences and opinions, and then use our imaginations.

(*Above*) Servants made up a quarter of London's 18th-century population. In Edward Penny's *City Shower* the maid so vigorously twirling her mop is wearing her mistress's cast-off clothes.

In 1771 Marlow painted the busy waterfront, west of Fresh Wharf. On the skyline are Westminster Abbey, the Banqueting Hall and York Water Tower. The Adelphi is under construction to the right.

A carpenter's rule, plane and blade, excavated at Cutler Street.

Sifting the Evidence

It is with surviving objects that the problem of imbalance in our picture of life in the 18th century first arises. Goods were being produced and sold in London as never before, but those which have found their way into museums, auction rooms and private collections tend to represent the upper end of the market. Some objects survive by accident. Many more survive because they are preserved for the value of their raw materials or the beauty of their appearance. The everyday items which can be most evocative of life in the past are very often missing from contemporary collections. This is partly because they were used until they fell apart or were broken beyond repair, but it is also the case that until fairly recently they held little interest for most museum curators, scholars and collectors. However, as historians have become increasingly interested in the lives of 'ordinary' people, they have turned to other sources of evidence. To discover 18th-century London's true character, we must look beyond museums to this great wealth of other material, which is to be found anywhere from excavated cesspits to court records.

Though archaeology is often associated with the excavation and study of a past which is considerably more remote than the 1700s, it can help to reveal the most recent history of a city which has changed as rapidly as London has. Excavation of city rubbish tips and manufacturing sites has brought to light objects of which few other examples appear to have survived, and has provided useful information about various manufacturing processes, which becomes particularly valuable when combined with written evidence. This

(*Right*) Museum of London archaeologists have recently unearthed debris from a waterfront porcelain manufactory at Limehouse. As a result, it is at last possible to identify the porcelain made there.

method also confirms such things as the diet of Londoners almost three centuries ago – not least the vast quantities of oysters that were apparently consumed!

When objects are considered in conjunction with other kinds of evidence a more balanced picture begins to emerge. For instance, wills and inventories list the material possessions of people from a range of backgrounds and from these it has been possible to establish that less affluent Londoners were acquiring more and more material goods as the century progressed, just as the middle and upper classes were doing. Shop and workshop inventories list the stock-in-trade of a wide range of tradespeople, indicating not only what was actually made and sold, but also the changes in fashion and demand.

Court and prison records are essential to our understanding of a wide range of issues. Obviously such records note the kinds of crimes that were committed and the penalties they drew, from fines to execution or transportation. But both prosecution and defence evidence can also contain detailed accounts of living conditions and of the social and financial circumstances of both defendant and witnesses. Prison records of various kinds reveal a great deal about the conditions under which people were kept, the food they were given or bought, and the sort of work they were expected to do.

Many of the more sensational and gory crimes were described in newspapers and magazines, complete with illustrations! These same publications can highlight almost every aspect of, and attitude towards, life in 18th-century London, from the state of the pavements to the latest scientific invention or theatrical production. Provincial newspapers also give some indication of the way people outside London responded to its attractions and its dangers. Paintings and drawings, prints, pamphlets of all kinds from political satires to lists of brothels, religious tracts, private and business letters, diaries, advertisements, tradecards and bills: all contribute to our picture of London as it was two centuries ago.

A sense of the noise, chaos and crowds of City streets can be gained from William Hogarth's engraving, *The Enraged Musician*.

A Growing Population

London's population doubled during the 1700s, reaching just under one million by the time of the 1801 census. The increase was considerably more rapid in the second half of the century; indeed, one or two commentators in earlier decades expressed concern that the city's population might become dangerously low. This doubling of numbers sounds dramatic, but it was matched by an equivalent increase in the population of England and Wales as a whole. Thus, in both 1700 and 1800 just over 10 per cent of the nation's people lived in the capital city.

In 1700, the population of Paris was only slightly lower than that of London, but by 1801 twice as many people lived in London as in Paris. Ten per cent of the English and Welsh lived in the English capital, while Paris was home to only 2 per cent of the French. This suggests that London was the greater magnet to all kinds of trading, manufacturing, commercial, governmental and social activities, one reason for this being that there were a number of other populous cities in France, whereas Norwich and Bristol, England's next largest towns, were small in comparison to London.

London's expansion through the 18th century is shown below. The plan is based on maps of 1720, 1746 and 1792–9.

Extent of built-up areas in eighteenth-century London based on maps of:
- 1792–9
- 1746
- 1720

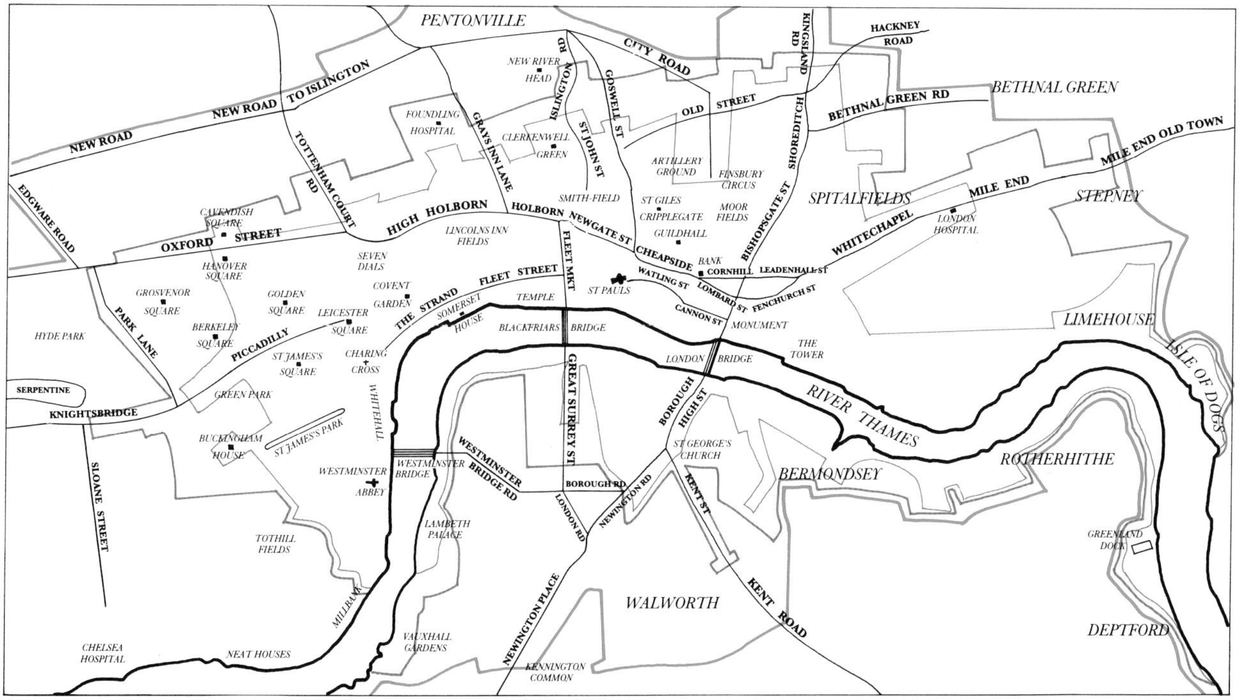

It has been estimated that within the boundaries of the medieval city walls, the population rose from about 80,000 in 1700 to around 87,000 by the middle of the century. After this numbers began to decline as merchants moved their homes and sometimes their workshops out to the new suburbs. Most 18th-century Londoners, therefore, settled outside the confines of the old City, living in the City of Westminster, in parishes along the river to the east, to the south of London Bridge and westwards towards the newly developing areas around the Court of St James.

City of Immigrants

In common with most large towns of the time, London's mortality rate was dramatically higher than its birth rate. The capital's population levels were kept up by large numbers of immigrants who settled on a permanent, or more commonly, on a temporary basis. Burrington suggested in 1757 that 'not above one in twenty of shop and alehouse keepers, journeymen and labourers ... were either born or served their apprenticeships in town. It is very probable that two thirds of the grown persons at any one time in London come from distant parts.'

'Distant parts' meant anywhere from America to Oxford as far as native Londoners were concerned. Most of those who settled in the city came from other parts of England and Wales, particularly from the home counties and East Anglia. Agricultural enclosures and the decline of home-based industries in the countryside drove thousands to London in search of employment. This pattern altered slightly as the century progressed and the growing industrial centres of the Midlands and the North began to draw local unemployed and dispossessed in their own areas.

Those who settled in London joined people of many nationalities who had come for a variety of political, economic and religious reasons. Native Londoners were notoriously prejudiced against most foreign immigrants, and mercilessly exploited less sophisticated people from the provinces. Foreign immigrants, therefore, tended to live and work together in specific areas, forming communities partly for cultural and religious reasons, and partly for self-protection.

Peter Lely's portrait of Charlotte Fitzroy and an Indian servant. Many Indians arrived in London as a result of the trading and colonising activities of the East India Company.

YORK CITY ART GALLERY

(*Right*) An early 19th-century view of the Bevis Marks Synagogue, built in 1701 to serve the Spanish and Portuguese Sephardic community. From a painting by Isaac Mendes Belisario.

THE JEWISH MUSEUM

In the first plate of Hogarth's series *The Harlot's Progress*, an innocent country girl arrives to work as a servant but is lured instead into a life of prostitution.

Ignatius Sancho, painted in 1768 by Thomas Gainsborough. He arrived in England on a slave ship, became butler to the Duchess of Montagu, and subsequently owned a fashionable grocery business.

Foreign Communities

Sephardic Jews from Spain and Portugal had settled in London in the 17th century and were by this time respected and often wealthy citizens. Political disturbances and anti-Semitic feeling in Europe caused other Jews to flee to London in the hope of support from the established Sephardic community, something which was not always forthcoming. By the end of the century there were an estimated 20,000 Jewish people in London, most of them living and working to the east of the City. There were fears that Jewish immigrants would deprive English labourers of work by undercutting established wage rates and in many trades the apprenticeship of Jews to Christian masters was forbidden. Also settled in the East End was a growing, transient community of Lascars, people from the East Indies who manned the East India Company's ships.

Black people from Africa, the Caribbean and the Americas made up only a small proportion of the immigrant community in the 18th century. Perhaps because they were few in number, Londoners seem to have found them less threatening than some other immigrant groups. Some had come as hired hands on ships from the North American colonies. Others had arrived as slaves or been brought to meet the demand for black servants as accessories to fashionable living, and were advertised for sale or exchange in the newspapers. There are many records of their being ill-treated and abandoned. One such case, that of the slave James Somerset in 1771–2, led to Lord Chief Justice Mansfield's historic but often disregarded ruling that 'as soon as any slave sets his foot upon English ground he becomes free.'

Irish immigrants came to London in large numbers. They settled mainly in the poorer parishes of Holborn, Marylebone, Stepney and Whitechapel. Many contributed to the pool of unskilled seasonal labourers, working mainly in various branches of the building trade and as agricultural labourers. Others found occasional work in the textile industry. In 1736 there were riots over the use of cheap Irish labour in the Spitalfields silk industry, where the Irish linen weavers had turned to silk weaving and were accepting lower rates than local workers.

Also living and working in Spitalfields were French Huguenots, Protestants who had fled religious persecution in the late 17th century. Like the established Jewish community they maintained strong cultural and religious traditions, providing schools, hospitals and charity for their own people and supporting their own churches. Although the majority were engaged in the silk industry a number made their mark as highly skilled craftspeople and decorative artists.

There were fewer Scots than Irish in London, and they were geographically less concentrated. Like the Irish, though, they tended to find seasonal employment and to be amongst the lower paid workers. Many Welsh people were engaged in the dairy trade or involved in cattle droving and livestock trading.

The 1730s silk for this dress was produced in Spitalfields, where French Huguenot weavers and craftspeople had settled late in the 17th century.

The Hungry City

Provision of food for London's growing population placed increasing demands on agricultural production in the provinces. Occasionally, this led to shortages in the area of production and consequently to food riots. According to Daniel Defoe, writing in the 1720s, 'this whole kingdom, as well the people as the land ... are employed to furnish something ... to support the City of London with provisions.'

Cattle for London's markets were driven from as far away as Wales, and it was necessary to protect their hooves with iron shoes such as these.

The daytime bustle of Covent Garden Market, painted by John Collet in 1770–80. At night, the area attracted patrons of theatres, coffee houses, taverns and brothels.

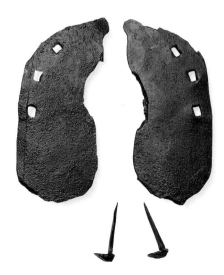

The highly profitable market that London offered led to a constant search for more efficient methods of farming, greater crop yields and improved animal breeds. More agricultural enclosures followed and so more country people moved to London in search of work … and they, of course, needed to eat. The number of 'middlemen' such as wholesalers, cattle fatteners and corn factors (dealers) increased considerably and some established extremely profitable monopolies.

By 1800, as many as 100,000 head of cattle were driven annually from the Welsh borders and the Midlands to be fattened in the home counties and suburbs for London consumption. Thousands of tons of grain were shipped up the Thames from east coast ports or brought by road from Kent and Essex. Suffolk and Essex provided much of the capital's dairy produce but cheese also came from as far away as Cheshire, as did salt. Vegetables and fruit were grown in market gardens and orchards to the west and south of London.

Chickens, turkeys and geese came from Norfolk and Suffolk. Besides the catches of the London fleet, fish also arrived from east coast ports and from Tyneside. Yarmouth herrings and Essex oysters were cheap and plentiful, and could be considered the equivalent 'street foods' to today's hamburgers and hot-dogs. Milk came from London-kept cows, but like tea and the increasingly popular white bread it was subject to adulteration: it was often skimmed, diluted and dirty. Wealthier customers preferred milk sold directly from cows led through the streets and squares. Widely available alternatives to milk or water were gin and beer, available from over 10,000 licensed (and unlicensed!) outlets.

Established major wholesale markets supported an increasing number of lesser local markets and supplied street traders and shopkeepers. Smithfield dealt in meat, Covent Garden in vegetables and fruit, Billingsgate in fish, Queenhythe in grain and Leadenhall in poultry. The streets around these markets became increasingly congested and there were frequent complaints of noise and stench. Porters at the principal markets were licensed and regular employment there was a jealously defended privilege.

Imported foodstuffs increased in popularity and coffee, tea and sugar were established items by the late 1600s. Chocolate became the fashionable drink in 18th-century London; at one point in the 1730s the household of politician Robert Walpole was consuming more than 1000 lb (500 kg) per year! Wine came from France, oranges and lemons from Portugal, and limes, molasses and rum from the West Indies. Small quantities of exotic fruits, including pineapples, were also grown in glasshouses to the west of London: the contents of the city's lay-stalls were brought by river to provide deep beds of the necessary rich manure.

Compared with their provincial counterparts, working Londoners generally ate well, although food purchase still took up a large part of the weekly budget for many people. Prices for 'non-essential' items such as sugar and tea dropped by as much as 10 per cent in the first half of the century, whereas labourers' wages increased slightly over the same period. Bread, cheese and beer formed a typical breakfast, with a main meal of meat (often fatty pork), dumplings or vegetables. This might be bought from one of the city's many 'take-away' cookshops.

Wealthier people ate more meat, particularly beef, and several fashionable households employed French cooks. On the whole, however, foreign visitors were no more impressed with standards of cooking in London than they are today!

Fellowship Porters were licensed to carry goods sold by measure, such as corn, coal and fish. Each wore a leather tally, with thongs to record the number of completed jobs.

Health and Death

It is likely that only about 40 per cent of those born in London during the early 1700s survived to the age of fifteen, although this figure rose to around 60 per cent by the end of the century. At times the death rate was even more dramatic: it has been estimated that between 1730 and 1750 as many as three-quarters of London-born children died before the age of five. Certain diseases such as smallpox, typhus and influenza were constant threats, and there were also periodic epidemics of individual diseases. However, by the

St George's Hospital was built near Hyde Park so that patients could benefit from the 'country' air. By the 1740s it could accommodate up to 250 charity patients.

end of the century the London death rate fell significantly, partly as a result of the availability of vaccination against smallpox and better general health care.

On the whole, though, the century saw vastly improved concern and provision for the health of Londoners, largely because of private philanthropy. Five new hospitals were founded: Westminster (1720), Guy's (1724), St George's (1733), London (1740) and Middlesex (1745). A number of specialised hospitals were also established, such as the 'lying-in' or maternity hospitals.

Wealthy benefactors were also responsible for the setting up of public dispensaries. These dealt with outpatients only, diagnosing illnesses and prescribing drugs, and it has been estimated that by the end of the century as many as 50,000 people were being treated in these centres. Used mainly by poorer people, London's dispensaries also tended to be centres for the activities of those who hoped to improve the moral as well as physical health of their clients.

There were also gradual improvements in the provision of care for the mentally sick. The Bethlem Hospital (Bedlam), where the inmates were on display like animals to wealthy and fashionable sightseers, closed to paying visitors in 1766. A number of private asylums opened in the suburbs and were often run on more enlightened and humane lines, although this was not always the case: there are accounts of such places being used as 'dumping-grounds' for unwanted but perfectly sane people, often women who had outlived their usefulness as wealthy or attractive marriageable commodities.

A silver toothbrush, tongue-scraper and box of dental powder might go some way towards lessening the effects of a rich diet and heavy drinking.

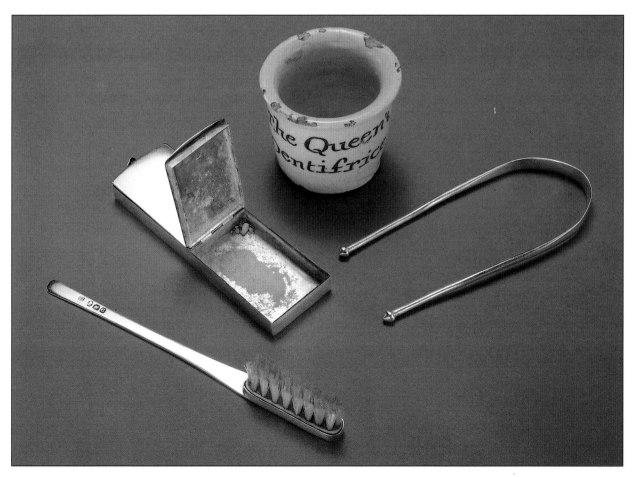

Not all 18th-century remedies were effective. These bottles contained medicines sold by reputable pharmacists but 'quack' doctors also did a roaring trade in coloured water and flour pills.

A death was marked by the distribution of elaborate mourning cards and jewellery. This card records the death in 1792 of Sir Joshua Reynolds, painter and first president of the Royal Academy. Also shown here is a commemorative pendant.

Graveyards in the City were obviously limited in their capacity and became terribly overcrowded. The wealthy could afford to be buried in stone or brick vaults, but for many poor people the only available burial was in a paupers' grave, which often remained open until it had been filled with a number of bodies. It then became a health risk, as did the shallow graves in the City churchyards.

Religious Life

For many Londoners, church attendance was largely a matter of habit, and in fashionable parishes it was often seen as a social rather than a devotional exercise: 'Some pretty young ladies in mobs popped in here and there about the church,' wrote the essayist Steele, 'clattering the pew door after them, and squatting in whispers behind their fans.' Most people seldom, if ever, attended church services.

Men such as John and Charles Wesley and George Whitefield set out to combat such laxity and to encourage more people to lead religiously active lives, and in 1738, John Wesley began preaching in London churches. However, his growing criticism of the Established Church meant that from 1739 he was forced to begin preaching out of doors. He and Whitefield addressed gatherings of thousands on Blackheath and Moorfields. In November of 1739, Wesley preached at a disused foundry near Moorfields, a 'vast uncouth heap of ruins' which he bought the following year for £115. This remained his headquarters until 1778, when a new chapel was opened in the City Road. Other chapels opened in Southwark (1743), Spitalfields (1750) and Wapping (1764). Worship was enlivened by the many new hymns which the Wesleys wrote for congregational use. Wesley's Methodism appealed particularly to the trading and professional classes, whilst Whitefield attracted more radical and politically active congregations to his tabernacles in Moorfields and, from 1756, Tottenham Court Road.

The older dissenting groups – Presbyterians, Quakers, Baptists and Independents – increased their numbers during the 18th century but in London at least were less openly evangelical than the Methodists. Quakers, their lives guided by 'inner light' rather than organised worship, became particularly well regarded as business people of great honesty and integrity.

This sermon glass from St Alban's, Wood Street, may have limited the preacher to an hour, though he could have turned it over and continued for longer.

Roman Catholics led a rather less secure religious existence than did members of the dissenting groups, who were largely protected by the Toleration Act. It was difficult for Catholics to recruit new converts and anti-Catholic feeling periodically threatened their position. Many of them worshipped in private chapels or in those attached to foreign embassies such as the Sardinian Chapel in Duke Street, which was partially burnt by the mob during the anti-Catholic Gordon Riots of 1780.

The Sephardic Jews were served by the Bevis Marks Synagogue, and the larger Ashkenazim community worshipped at the Great Synagogue in Duke's Place. The Jewish community was never fully tolerated and the Jewish Naturalisation Act of 1753 had to be repealed the following year because of the popular opposition it aroused, particularly in London.

Other foreign communities maintained their own places of worship in London. There were more than twenty-five French Protestant churches for example, mainly in Spitalfields and Soho. Some translated the Anglican liturgy into French, whilst others conformed to the Genevan tradition.

This wooden model of a preacher in his pulpit belongs to Her Majesty the Queen.

George Whitefield (far right) and John Wesley (right) were London's most charismatic non-conformist preachers. They drew vast crowds, both at their chapels and in the open.

WESLEY'S CHAPEL

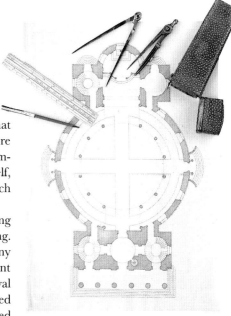

An Expanding City

Towards the end of the century, the writer Horace Walpole predicted that there would be 'one street from London to Brentford'. By 1800, there were approximately thirty-four square kilometres of densely packed houses and commercial premises, elegant terraces and public buildings. Within the city itself, there was the kind of perpetual demolition and rebuilding cycle to which Londoners of the late 20th century have become accustomed.

Following the Great Fire of 1666 there had been various plans for rebuilding the City along spacious continental lines, but none of them came to anything. This was partly because freeholders were anxious to hang on to the many small but very profitable parcels of land which they owned and were reluctant to sell in the interests of a 'grand scheme'. So the old City retained its medieval street plan to a great extent, with reconstruction and repair of fire-damaged buildings. Such large-scale building as did occur in the City was concentrated in the public and commercial sectors.

Foreign and provincial visitors, as well as Londoners themselves, expressed amazement at the speed and extent of the capital's growth; many wondered when and where it would stop. Tobias Smollet wrote in 1771: 'I am credibly informed that, in the space of seven years, eleven thousand new houses have been built in one quarter of Westminster, exclusive of what is daily added to other parts of this unwieldy metropolis. Pimlico and Knightsbridge are almost joined to Chelsea and Kensington and, if this infatuation continues for half a century, I suppose the whole county of Middlesex will be covered with brick.' It is important that we remind ourselves, however, that by 20th-century standards London was still a small city, from which it was comparatively easy to escape into open countryside.

There was plenty of work for architects in the expanding city. This rejected scheme was one of several put forward by James Gibbs for St Martin-in-the-Fields.

In spite of increasing urban sprawl, open countryside and farmland remained easily accessible to Londoners until the end of the century.

New Developments

Much of the energy of developers and speculative builders was concentrated on the squares and streets of the West End. Major periods of building activity coincided with periods of national prosperity and there were lulls at times of war or economic depression.

The earliest squares had been laid out in the previous century. Covent Garden Piazza (1631), St James's Square (1665) and Bloomsbury Square (1666) were inspired by continental models in Italy and France. Eighteenth-century developments were based mainly on the estates of major landowning families and were often named after them. They occupied land previously used for grazing, gardening and recreation, which meant that these activities were pushed further out into the suburbs.

Some squares had a particular social identity. Hanover Square, developed on the accession of the Elector of Hanover as George I in 1714, was occupied by the Whig aristocracy and by military officers. Cavendish Square, developed between 1717 and 1728, was home to Tory politicians, whilst Bedford Square (1775–80) was close to the Inns of Court and provided convenient housing for lawyers.

The appearance of the more fashionable squares reflected current architectural fashions. Landowners and developers of the major squares often employed eminent architects to design them, or at least to oversee their planning.

Many of London's new housing developments were undertaken by speculative builders who would sometimes construct the shell of a house on a leased

Hanover Square, begun in 1714, was the first of the great 18th-century squares. This engraving shows the view north towards Hampstead and Highgate.

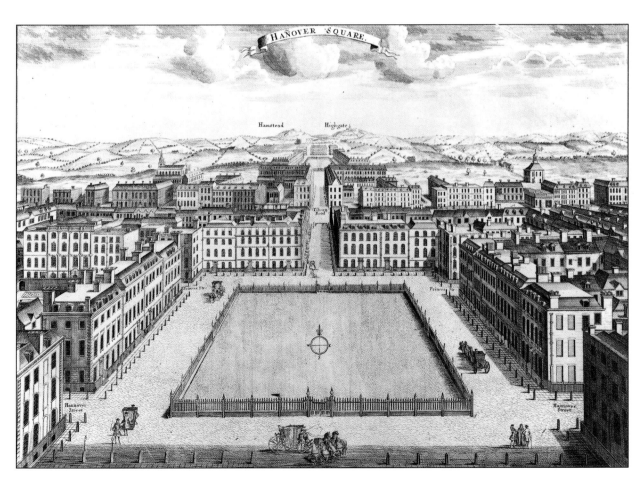

site and then sell it on before the ground rent became due. Such rapidly erected houses occasionally collapsed before completion, but those that did appear sound were then finished by their new owners to their own taste.

The Adelphi, developed on the Thames riverfront by the Adam brothers between 1768 and 1772, was one of the most ambitious speculative building projects in 18th-century London. It consisted of a terrace of elegant private houses raised to the level of the Strand above storage vaults and warehouses at river level. The houses, however, did not sell as well as had been expected and the Adam brothers were almost bankrupted by the project.

After the Great Fire of 1666, various Building Acts limited the use of timber in house-building, bricks became more widely used, and chains of brick kilns surrounded London. With the Palladian revival came a fashion for grey stocks, yellowish bricks made of London clay mixed with chalk. Other building materials included York, Purbeck and Portland stone, and woods such as English oak, fir from the American colonies and Scandinavia, and mahogany from the West Indies. Tiles, pantiles and, from the 1760s, slates were used for roofing. Window glass came by barge from Newcastle or from London glassworks.

One of the most interesting new building materials was Coade stone. A kind of terracotta, its precise composition remained a closely guarded secret. It was first made by George and Eleanor Coade at Lambeth in the late 1760s and its great attraction was that it could be cast into a wide range of ornamental and sculptural forms.

Coade's architectural ornaments were a comparatively cheap, quick and adaptable alternative to carved stonework. The Lambeth factory became a tourist attraction.

Although several famous people made their homes there, the Adam brothers' speculative Adelphi development almost bankrupted them.

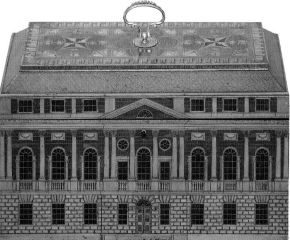

These inlaid tea caddies are representative of the kinds of houses in which wealthier Londoners made their homes.

Hogarth set *Gin Lane* in Seven Dials, one of the most densely populated and poverty-stricken areas of 18th-century London. Cheap and adulterated gin offered many people their only relief from appalling living conditions.

Middle-class Londoners lived in houses such as these, built in Cowley Street, Westminster, around 1720.

Poverty and Affluence

As the city grew, there developed a more marked separation of different social and economic classes than had previously existed. The 'City Within' – that is, the area inside the old walls – retained its traditional mix for the earlier part of the century, with extremely rich merchants living cheek by jowl with artisans and the very poor. Contemporary tax records suggest that as many as a third of the residents here fell into the highest tax brackets. Increasingly, though, the trend was towards segregation.

The City itself was ringed by parishes where most people were in the lowest tax groups or paid nothing at all. Growing numbers of bourgeois or middle-class Londoners were settling in the new suburbs to the north, northeast and south, whilst the aristocracy and the wealthy congregated in the spacious streets and squares being developed around the Court of St James to the west.

Probably the largest area of concentrated poverty, and thus one most feared by both Londoners and visitors, was Seven Dials, near Covent Garden. Here, together with servants, day labourers and porters catering to the needs of the wealthier adjoining areas, lived thieves, prostitutes and beggars.

Vivid impressions of the capital's different areas can be gained from contemporary descriptions. In 1712 Joseph Addison wrote in the *Spectator*: 'When I consider this great City in its several quarters and divisions, I look upon it as an aggregate of various nations distinguished from each other by their respective customs, manners and interests ...' In 1780, the German von Archenholz commented: 'The east end, especially along the shores of the Thames, consists of old houses, the streets there were narrow, dark and ill-paved ... the contrast between this and the west end is astonishing; the houses here are mostly new and elegant; the squares are superb, the streets straight and open ... If all London were as well built there would be nothing in the world to compare with it.'

Most Londoners lived in rather crowded conditions, however. In the City, a house would typically be occupied by several families, each paying rent to the leaseholder, whose family and business usually occupied the lower floors. In the poorest areas people often shared accommodation in a single room, using it at different times of the day.

Public Utilities

Before the Westminster Paving Acts of 1761 onwards, individual householders were responsible for paving and lighting the street outside their homes. Of course, this duty was often neglected or at best inconsistently fulfilled. Paving levels were hopelessly uneven and therefore dangerous, and roads all over the city were full of potholes. Under the Acts, however, Boards of Commissioners for each parish were made responsible for overseeing street-paving, which normally consisted of granite blocks laid in a bed of compacted earth.

As streets were repaired, drainage and sewer systems were improved and extended. The broad but often clogged and overflowing central gutter, which carried all kinds of waste, was replaced by narrower ones at the road's edges which emptied into underground drains. Domestic waste and sewage was collected from private cesspits in special carts by the 'night-soil' men. It was then taken to 'lay-stalls' on the city's fringes or on the riverfront, from where much of it went to manure market gardens or to be used in the brickmaking industry.

An observer writing in 1783 remarked that beneath the pavements were 'vast subterraneous sewers to convey away the waste water ... and at a lesser depth are buried wooden pipes that supply every house plentifully with water,

Although a few people enjoyed the luxury of a flushing water closet, most had to make do with chamber pots. These could be highly ornamented or, like this pewter one, functionally plain.

Crossing the city's dirty, unevenly paved and ill-repaired streets could be a hazardous business, as this gently satirical print suggests.

A. Grant del.

CROSSING A DIRTY STREET.

A nightman's brass plaque. Nightmen, besides emptying cesspits and disposing of waste, often worked as chimney sweeps during the day.

Chelsea Waterworks in 1752. The two Newcomen beam engines installed here, in 1742 and 1747, pumped water to reservoirs in Green Park and Hyde Park. The site is now occupied by Victoria Station.

This small manual fire engine was built in 1735 for use at Windsor Castle. Larger versions were used by parishes and fire insurance companies.

conducted by leaden pipes into kitchens or cellars three times a week for the trifling expense of three shillings per quarter.' Water was supplied by a number of private companies, who pumped water from the Thames or drew it from sources to the north of the city into collecting ponds and reservoirs and then piped it into customers' houses. Up to a third of piped water was lost through leakage!

Public conduits, which for centuries had provided Londoners with free water, were allowed to deteriorate. They were being replaced as early as 1725 by unreliable 'street pumps and wells where poor people who cannot afford to pay for water can obtain it for nothing. Absolutely none is drunk. The lower classes, even the pauper, do not know what it is to quench their thirst with water.' Many of them drank cheap gin instead.

Water for quenching fires, which in spite of stricter building regulations since the 1666 Great Fire were alarmingly frequent, was provided mainly by wooden fire engines. Parish fire-fighting services were highly unreliable and those who could afford to subscribed to the increasing number of private insurance companies. Firemen, usually Thames watermen, wore a distinctive livery and badge, and rivalry between companies was intense. Fire marks attached to buildings showed which company the owner or tenant was insured with. Buildings occasionally burned to the ground because firemen from one company refused to save premises insured with a rival, rather than because there was no engine at all in attendance.

Street lighting, until the 1761 Acts largely the responsibility of private citizens, improved as the century progressed. In poorly lit areas 'link-men' and boys carrying pitch torches guided people through the streets. In better class areas householders provided whale-oil lamps outside their properties and organised street-lighting systems were established. By 1780 'in Oxford Road [Street] alone there were more lamps than in all the city of Paris.' This may have been an exaggeration, but it does indicate the impression that London's comparatively well-lit streets made on visitors.

Transport

Severe and increasing congestion on London's streets meant that it was usually quicker to take a sedan chair or to travel on foot or by boat. Wheeled vehicles merely joined the crush of barrows, waggons and coaches already packing the narrow streets in the older parts of the city. Sedan chairs could be hired from ranks, much as taxis can be today, and could be carried into the hallways of larger houses. Chair fares were theoretically fixed, but overcharging was fairly common.

Also operating a fixed-fare structure were the thousands of licensed watermen carrying passengers on the Thames in their wherries. The river was still a major thoroughfare at the beginning of the 19th century, despite the opening of the Westminster and Blackfriars bridges in 1750 and 1769 respectively. Before Westminster Bridge brought easy access to the developing area south of the Thames, horse-drawn traffic crossing west of London Bridge used a ferry which ran between Lambeth Palace and Millbank (Horseferry Road).

Moving around on foot could be hazardous. The streets were littered with all kinds of obstructions – garbage, animals, traders' barrows and so on –

Licensed waterman's arm badge. Many watermen also worked as firemen for the fire insurance companies.

Short-haul coaches served places fairly close to London and were the forerunners of 19th-century omnibuses.

GREENWICH   CHARING ✠ CROSS   WOOLWICH

The ROYAL SAILOR.

Road travel was a dangerous business. Lord Eglington, for example, was robbed of his portmanteau and 50 guineas on Hounslow Heath in 1750 – even though he was armed with a blunderbuss!

and there was always the danger of having your pocket picked. Lighting was very patchy in many areas and on moonless nights pedestrians could hire link-boys to light the way. Unfortunately, the link-boys were sometimes in league with footpads and thieves, with inevitable consequences for the unsuspecting citizen!

As the city spread, the demand for horse-drawn transport increased. Hackney carriages capable of carrying two or three passengers operated within the city itself. Destinations just beyond London were served by short-stage coaches, forerunners of the omnibus. A popular method of private transport was the post-chaise, introduced in the 1740s. A light, covered carriage, it was ideal for urban use and for rapid journeys generally.

Roads out of London were poorly maintained and dangerous: in a single week in 1720, all the stage coaches coming into the City from Surrey were robbed! The *Gentleman's Magazine* observed in 1756 that the road beyond Aldgate 'resembled a stagnant lake of deep mud'. In the latter part of the century, Turnpike Trusts began to undertake the improvement and maintenance of major routes out of the capital, collecting tolls at the principal exit points. From the 1780s new light-weight mail coaches travelled the turnpikes free of charge. They left from the General Post Office in Lombard Street, keeping strictly to timetable and revolutionising the previously unreliable postal system. From the coaching inns, waggons and coaches carried goods and passengers to all parts of the country. There was fierce competition on many routes, with operators undercutting one another on charges and journey times.

By the beginning of the 19th century there was a new and efficient method of transporting goods and raw materials into and out of the capital. A network of canals joined the Thames with the rivers Trent, Severn and Mersey. The great port and commercial centre of London thus had direct water transport links with several of the country's major new manufacturing and trading centres.

Whitechapel Turnpike. By the end of the century, tolls funded the maintenance of all such main roads out of the capital.

Local Government

Administration of local government in 18th-century London was complex. In the City, two central governing bodies were based at the Guildhall. The Upper Court was made up of aldermen, often holding purchased office for life, and the much larger Court of Common Council consisted of more than 200 'freemen' elected annually from the livery companies. The livery companies, which had developed from the medieval trade guilds, were increasingly involved in social and philanthropic activities, rather than with the preservation of professional standards and the protection of members' rights.

Responsibility for most of the day-to-day administration of local government, however, rested with the parishes. Parish vestries had functions and commitments similar to those of present-day local councils. Members of 'close' vestries were freeholders (people with property rights) who held office for life. 'Open' vestries elected their officers annually from amongst all the parish's ratepayers. Both systems were open to abuse and corruption, with offices being sold to the highest bidder or being granted to men who then 'sub-let' them to their own supporters.

Each parish officer had particular responsibilities. Churchwardens looked after the maintenance of the church itself and organised the religious side of parish life. The Constable executed warrants, made arrests and attended court hearings. In most parishes he was also responsible for the provision of the parish watch and for raising the parish militia, an armed guard which could be called upon in times of local and national emergency. The Surveyor ensured that householders met their obligations to pave and light the areas outside their homes, and was often required to organise the collection of rates and local taxes.

It is important to stress the lack of uniformity in the provision of services by different London parishes. Some were run by thoughtful and enlightened officials, whilst others were controlled by unscrupulous and greedy men who used their official posts for their own ends. Outside the City itself, the existence of over 300 local government and parish bodies meant that the provision of even the most basic London-wide public services was difficult to organise.

Lead boundary markers were attached to buildings so that the limits of a parish's responsibility could be clearly defined. This one comes from St Stephen's, Coleman Street.

(*Right*) Thomas Rowlandson's watercolour of a nightwatchman on his rounds draws attention to the inefficiency of parish law enforcement. In the background two burglars are brazenly going about their business.

(*Below*) In addition to his lantern and club, the watchman might also have carried a wooden rattle.

(*Far left*) Parish constables were entitled to carry official truncheons such as these. They were often elaborately decorated.

Providing for the Poor

One of the most important of the parish officers was the Overseer of the Poor, who distributed parish relief and arranged for the return of as many paupers as possible to their 'parishes of origin'. Legislation over the previous two centuries stipulated that destitute people became the responsibility of the parish in which they were found unless the parish of their birth or early residence could be discovered.

(*Left*) A popular print of Thomas Coram, outside the Foundling Hospital. Handel and Hogarth were amongst the eminent people who took an active interest in the work of the hospital.

Painted figures of children from the Baynard Castle Ward School. A surprisingly large number of city children were educated in charitable institutions such as this.

The return of poor people to other parishes was of great importance in London, where the constant influx of immigrants from outside the city could easily stretch local resources to breaking point. Pregnant women were particularly liable to removal, since they represented two potential clients for parish relief: there are records of their being dumped across the boundary into a neighbouring parish while in the final stages of labour!

(*Left*) Pins produced in workhouses and prisons were usually sold on to an outside tradesman, who would pack and sell them under his own name.

Sir John Fielding examining a prisoner at the Bow Street public office. He was blind and generally wore a black band around his eyes.

As policing became more organised, detection methods became more scientific.

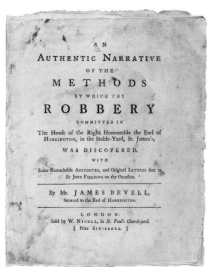

The Overseer was also responsible for arranging the housing, education and apprenticeship of destitute children and orphans. Very small children were lodged with wet-nurses in the country. After parish workhouses had been established by Act of Parliament in 1722, children who no longer needed nursing went to live in the workhouses where, together with the adult inmates, they produced goods such as pins which were sold to offset parish expenses.

Education of parish children was seldom more than the minimum needed to place them as apprentices with tradespeople. The parish apprenticeship scheme, like so many other aspects of parish administration, was open to exploitation and abuse. Many parish Overseers placed children in areas of high labour shortage outside London, where they provided cheap labour for employers who were happy to bribe parish officials to turn a blind eye to the children's working and living conditions. Those children placed with London masters were seldom given more than basic training.

A growing number of philanthropic organisations concerned themselves with the welfare of poor people. They evolved partly as a response to a general sense of the inferiority of London's institutions as compared with those on the Continent, particularly in Paris, where poor relief was traditionally provided by the great 'hospitals'. The activities of these new institutions, and of a growing number of socially concerned writers, were generally directed towards particular groups of poor people, such as prostitutes or children.

The Foundling Hospital is probably the best known of these newer philanthropic foundations. In 1739 Captain Thomas Coram was granted a charter for the hospital's establishment. Its first premises were in Hatton Garden, from where it moved in 1747 to a new building in Lamb's Conduit Fields. At first, the mothers of unwanted children drew lots for the admission of their babies. Later, Parliament granted the hospital financial aid provided that all babies under eight weeks old were accepted. A large basket was left outside the building, where babies could be left anonymously. They were sent to the country until they were five and then returned to the hospital to be educated and trained for a range of fairly humble occupations.

Police and Prisons

Crime in London increased at times of trade depression and harvest failure. Most theft was of food and necessary goods and there were comparatively few 'professional' thieves. The number of hanging offences increased during the century but the number of executions for such crimes actually decreased. Judges, magistrates and juries were clearly aware of the absurdity of a system which treated a handkerchief thief as seriously as it did a mass-murderer! Some of them built up a considerable popular following by granting pardons and reprieves, and during the last quarter of the century over half of those condemned to death were pardoned or were transported rather than hanged.

Not all magistrates and judges were enlightened, however, and there was a great deal of corruption at all levels of law enforcement. So-called 'trading justices' bought their offices and then recovered their expenses by collecting bribes. Horace Walpole maintained that 'the greatest criminals of this town are the officers of justice.' The notorious Jonathan Wild used his position as a thief-taker and 'returner of stolen goods' to cover his more profitable activities as a gang leader and fence!

For the first part of the century there was no effective centrally organised police force. Neighbourhood policing was based on a system of constables and watchmen, who relied heavily on the support of public-spirited and often rather self-righteous citizens. Shopkeepers seem to have been particularly active in observing and reporting such crimes as petty theft and prostitution, no doubt because they were concerned with keeping up the tone of their neighbourhood.

It was left to a few concerned individuals to make the first attempts at founding a London-wide police force. In 1749 the magistrate and writer Henry Fielding and his brother John established a force of officers, based at Bow Street, who became known as the 'Bow Street Runners'. They were paid one guinea a week and a share in the rewards for successful prosecutions, but such central funding as there was tended to be unreliable.

Another magistrate, Patrick Colquhoun, represented many other reformers at the end of the century. He identified problems ranging from the lack of a proper police force to the severity of sentences for minor crimes and an inadequate prison system. In the late 1790s he set up the Thames or Marine Police, a force which was to be the first step in the direction of a centrally organised London policing system. He was also concerned with establishing a more rational and less corrupt prison system.

Gaol fever possibly killed as many condemned prisoners as the hangman. Prisons were often privately owned and run on a profit-making basis. The sale of better accommodation and other privileges meant that some prisoners

(*Below*) Newgate Gaol was vast and forbidding. Few escaped and many went on to transportation or hanging. The Old Bailey stands on the same site.

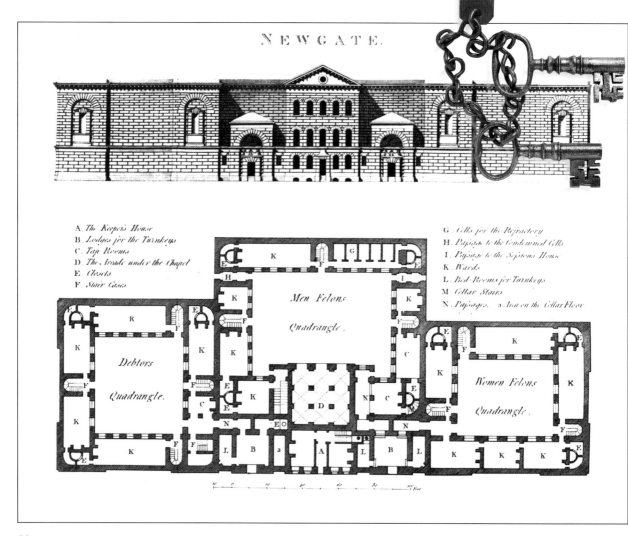

NEWGATE.

A. The Keeper's House
B. Lodges for the Turnkeys
C. Tap Rooms
D. The Arcade under the Chapel
E. Closets
F. Stair Cases

G. Cells for the Refractory
H. Passage to the Condemned Cells
I. Passage to the Sessions House
K. Wards
L. Bed-Rooms for Turnkeys
M. Cellar Stairs
N. Passages, also on the Cellar Floor

Debtors Quadrangle.

Men Felons Quadrangle.

Women Felons Quadrangle.

(Left) The pine walls of the Wellclose Square prison bear graffiti, cut in the 1750s and 1780s.

(Below left) The keys to Newgate's burying ground, the last home of those who died of gaol fever, or who committed suicide before their sentence could be executed.

The London Corresponding Society numbered many self-educated, radical artisans and tradesmen amongst its politically concerned members.

George I was not particularly popular with the citizens of London. This marble bust, of about 1732, is attributed to the workshop of Michael Rysbrack.

lived comparatively comfortably whilst others existed in shockingly over-crowded and unhealthy conditions. Whole families went to live in the Fleet prison when the principal breadwinner was imprisoned for debt, whilst debtors in the King's Bench prison were allowed out during the day to carry on limited trading or business activities. On the whole, London's many prisons tended to reinforce rather than reform criminal behaviour and an increasing number of philanthropists, such as John Howard, concerned themselves with trying to improve the situation.

Politics and Revolution

On the whole Londoners were politically well informed and took considerable interest in both local and national events. This interest was particularly marked amongst artisans, and several working mens' study groups, debating clubs and societies such as the London Corresponding Society were established in London during the course of the century.

Londoners' reactions to the new Hanoverian monarchy were varied but tended to be generally hostile. George I reluctantly took up the succession in 1714 but made little attempt to learn English or to endear himself to the citizens. The German kings were only tolerated as long as they kept out of politics. George III's political activities were seen by many as unconstitutional, and earned him the contempt of many Londoners, though his bouts of madness in later life and the reckless behaviour of his sons made people more sympathetic towards him at the end of his reign.

In political life, personality was all-important. Londoners made popular heroes of men whom they felt stood up for the rights of the individual. One such was the radical MP John Wilkes, whose stormy career between 1763 and 1774 earned him an enormous popular following. On several occasions the London mob rose in his support and the streets resounded to cries of 'Wilkes and Liberty'.

Both houses of Parliament were corrupt, as was the electoral system. Elections excited strong popular feeling even when people did not entirely grasp the issues involved. The Middlesex elections of 1768, when Wilkes was elected, and the riotous 1784 Westminster election which saw the victory of Charles James Fox, were both won by personalities as much as policies.

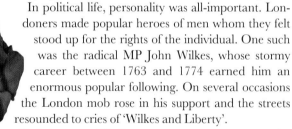

Londoners' reactions to political events abroad depended very much upon the degree to which their lives were affected by them. City merchants and tradesmen tended to side with the rebellious American colonists against an unpopular government which they felt was mismanaging national and city interests. Radicals supported the colonists as loyal, ill-treated subjects. On the other hand, loss of the colonies led to loss of trade and to the collapse of banks, and Samuel Johnson attacked the rebels as 'a race of convicts'.

The French Revolution also brought mixed responses. To begin with many Londoners welcomed it as an equivalent to England's Glorious Revolution of 1688. The storming of the Bastille was widely reported and was soon re-enacted at Astley's Amphitheatre. After the execution of Louis XVI, however, fears grew that the London mob might become similarly powerful. In response to London radicalism Edmund Burke wrote his *Reflections on the Revolution in France*, which warned of the dangers of rampant republicanism. The war with France which followed was unpopular with ordinary Londoners. Its progress was slow, it disrupted trade and threatened livelihoods, and the mob made attacks on the houses of London recruiting officers.

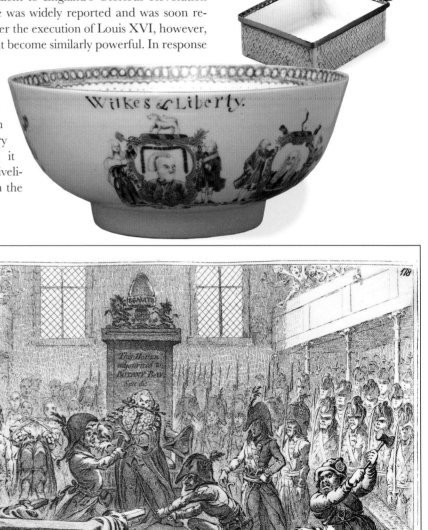

(*Left*) This Battersea enamel souvenir box carries a portrait of Robert Walpole, the country's first (and highly corrupt) prime minister. It was made around 1755.

(*Below left*) The popular radical MP John Wilkes is commemorated in the decoration of this punchbowl, dating from 1768.

(*Far left*) James Gillray's satire warns of the consequences of a successful French invasion for the English parliament.

During the anti-Catholic Gordon Riots of 1780, the London mob set fire to Newgate Gaol, most of which had to be rebuilt.

The London Mob

The inhabitants of the City of London had for centuries been a thorn in the flesh of the monarchy. Their support was vital if money was to be raised for government projects, particularly in wartime. Often, however, the citizens opposed the monarchy or Parliament and at such times they showed their disapproval by banding together in a vast unruly mob and taking to the streets in riotous protest. By the 18th century the London mob was of particular concern to the government not only because it was so volatile, but because the protesters were generally well-informed, fairly well-educated and independent citizens.

Mob demonstrations were often responses to purely local or partisan issues, sometimes linked to unrest in a particular trade or prejudice against a specific group of people, such as the Irish weavers. There were, however, occasions when the activities of the London mob affected national political events. For example, there was a genuine concern during the first two decades of the century that obvious anti-government factions in the city might link themselves to the Jacobite cause and bring about the downfall of the Hanoverian monarchy.

The most dramatic illustration of the power of the mob occurred in June 1780. Petitions made to Parliament by the anti-Catholic Protestant Association were not taken sufficiently seriously by the authorities, and protest rapidly escalated into violence. Under the leadership of Lord George Gordon a mob of between thirty and fifty thousand stormed through the city. Over several days of looting and arson, Newgate, Clerkenwell, the Fleet, the King's Bench

All the Prisoners to the amount of 300 were released this Night.

The Devastations occasioned by the **RIOTERS** *of* **LONDON** *Firing the New Goal of* **NEWGATE,** *and burning Mr. Akerman's Furniture, &c. June 6. 1780.*

Hamilton delin.   Thornton sc.

and Borough Clink prisons were burned and there was an unsuccessful attack on the Bank of England. Order was finally restored, but not before more than 400 people had been killed or wounded by government forces.

Whilst for many Londoners the anti-Catholic cause had genuinely been the principal motive for rioting, for many more it had simply provided an excuse for looting and assault. In the aftermath of the Gordon Riots some commentators suggested that lax moral standards and general resentment of property owners and government had as much to do with the uprising as had religious convictions. Rioting would continue, they believed, until something was done about the proper policing of the capital and the mob was restrained by law rather than 'official' violence.

The Gordon Riots offered the mob an excellent opportunity for widespread looting. Here, a house in Broad Street is being emptied of furniture.

Illustrations of newly discovered peoples appeared in journals and periodicals. This one is of 'a new Zealand Chief, curiously tataowed'.

Widening Horizons

There was a growing curiosity about the natural world which was both reflected and fostered by the establishment of learned societies and the achievements of 'amateur' scientists. The Royal Society of London had been founded in 1662, and its publication *Philosophical Transactions* reported on an increasing number of experiments, inventions and discoveries. New knowledge was collected and organised in encyclopaedias, dictionaries, museums and botanic gardens and was explained through public lectures and demonstrations.

London, and the nation as a whole, began to benefit from the interests of both societies and individuals. The surgeon Sir Hans Sloane, for example, left thousands of books, paintings, archaeological remains and natural history specimens. They were sold to the nation and formed the core collection of the British Museum, which opened in Montagu House, Bloomsbury, in 1759.

Travel books became very popular. Many included not only descriptions of newly discovered lands such as New Zealand but detailed accounts and illustrations of the people who lived there. There was a great deal of curiosity about people from different ethnic backgrounds, and showmen who brought such people to London often made a considerable amount of money by exhibiting them. Some travel books also contained charts and suggestions of trading possibilities. Accurate charting was difficult until the London clockmaker John Harrison produced his first marine chronometer in 1735. The subsequent perfection of chronometers revolutionised navigation and made possible very precise measurement of longitude.

Using the new navigational techniques, James Cook made three voyages of exploration to the Pacific between 1768 and 1776. Plants and other specimens collected on these voyages were sent to the Botanic Garden at Kew, where Frederick, Prince of Wales, had begun planting in the 1730s. His widow,

A London-made mechanical 'orrery' describing planetary motion. When the handle is turned, Mercury, Venus and the Earth rotate in their orbits around the Sun.

Princess Augusta, appointed William Aiton as the first director of the botanic specimen garden. He organised the garden according to the recently developed Linnaen system and by 1776 Kew was hailed as 'The Paradise of our World, where all plants are found that money or interest can procure'.

It was not primarily for the pleasure of collecting specimens, however, that most voyages of discovery were made. It was the desire to find new sources of raw materials and potential markets which lay at the root of the exploration undertaken by such trading concerns as the East India Company. For all their encouragement of scientific recording, what really motivated Captain Cook's backers was the expansion of British colonial interests. The foundations of the vast empire which Britain claimed in the 19th and early 20th centuries had been laid in the 16th century, but it was the activity of 18th-century London-based merchants and navigators which consolidated those early achievements.

Trade and Commerce

By the end of the 18th century, London had become the chief city of a rapidly expanding empire. Raw materials were imported from an increasing number of colonies, processed either in London or in the new manufacturing centres in the Midlands and the North and then exported to Europe and Asia or to the colonies. Goods produced in the colonies were shipped directly from London to European markets. It was possible to become extremely wealthy simply through speculation and shrewd investment and some of the greatest of England's country houses were built on the profits from such activity. London merchants married their children to impoverished aristocrats, trading fortunes for titles.

At the centre of all this trading activity was the Thames, which throughout the century continued to provide the economic lifeblood of London. Between 1720 and 1800 the trade of the Port of London tripled in volume. There was severe congestion all along the river, especially in the Upper Pool where up to 1800 vessels crowded into a mooring space suitable for about 500.

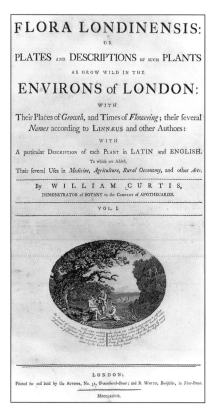

The title page of *Flora Londinensis*, a lavishly illustrated survey of London plants published in 1777.

Hogarth's *Marriage à la Mode* charts the disastrous course of an arranged marriage between a young nobleman and the daughter of a rich but miserly London merchant.

Larger ships had to lay downriver at Woolwich, Blackwall, Deptford and Limehouse, where they transferred their cargoes into the 3500 hoys and barges which added to the bustle of the river. As the volume of goods increased, ships sometimes had to wait for long periods before being unloaded, and cargoes often rotted or spoiled. Cargoes on which duty had to be paid were unloaded at the Legal Quays between London Bridge and the Tower of London, where warehousing and quay space were hopelessly inadequate.

By the mid-1790s overcrowding and expensive delays, together with an alarming level of theft and general dishonesty, had combined to threaten the existence not only of many merchants but of the port itself. However, the creation of the Marine Police – London's first police force – in 1798 soon curbed losses through theft, and proposals for the building of enclosed trading docks were carried out in the early 1800s.

Alongside the growth in trade, there was an enormous expansion in banking and other financial activity which set the pattern for London's position as an international centre for services – a position which it holds to this day. Many new professions emerged, particularly associated with money, stock and insurance dealing. A great deal of this new financial activity took place in some of the city's hundreds of coffee houses. Until the foundation of a Stock Exchange in 1773, for example, licensed stockbrokers worked from Jonathan's and Garraway's coffee houses, whilst Lloyd's Coffee House provided a base for insurance brokers.

The financial world suffered a serious setback in 1720. The South Sea Company agreed to redeem the government debt and offered government shareholders company stock in return for their investments. The resulting boom led to wild speculation, the Company was unable to pay a return, and panic set in. The 'South Sea Bubble' burst: many investors were ruined and many newly acquired fortunes were lost.'

Boitard's 1757 engraving of the Legal Quays shows the intense overcrowding of the port. Besides the forest of ships' masts, treadwheel cranes, Customs Officers and porters can be seen at work.

Industry and Workers

By 1800, most of the country's large-scale industrial production was established in the Midlands and the North. For much of the 18th century, however, almost every kind of manufacturing industry could be found in and around London, often on a comparatively small scale. Into the capital came raw materials or, more usually, partly processed goods for 'finishing'. Out through the port went finished goods to destinations in Britain, Europe and the colonies.

Most industries depended on a number of processes. Each stage was 'put out' to workers on piece-rates, with the master taking most of the profits and selling goods under his name. It was not unusual for all the different manufacturing and finishing processes to take place within a few streets, with children and apprentices acting as runners between one craftsperson and another. There was surprisingly little sweated labour since the kind of mass-market which depends on such practices did not really develop until the following century

English porcelain was made at Chelsea, Bow, Limehouse and Vauxhall in the mid-18th century. The Vauxhall factory at Lambeth, where this teapot was produced, operated between 1751 and 1764.

A watch made for the Turkish market by George Prior, around 1780–90. Swiss forgers capitalised on the high reputation of such London-made watches.

There were certain goods for which London was a particularly important centre of production. London-made clocks and watches, for example, had an international reputation and by mid-century were being exported as far as Turkey and even China. The industry became concentrated in Clerkenwell and operated in the way described above, with the many component parts being produced within a very small area.

An existing silk industry expanded with the influx of Huguenot refugees from the late 17th century onwards. Concentrated in the Spitalfields area, the industry produced silk fabrics, stockings and ribbons. Silk was extremely expensive; the many alterations made to a single garment, to suit both changing styles and figures, are evidence that these clothes were worn and valued for many years. Masters hired out looms to weavers whose families often lived and worked in a single room. Women and children were important in the silk industry, but as in most other areas they were the first to suffer in times of war or depression, to which the silk trade was particularly vulnerable.

Navigational and surgical instruments were also items for which London craftsmen were particularly famous. Compasses, telescopes, barometers, chronometers and sextants used by scientists, sailors and explorers all over the known world came from London workshops. There were major coach-building and shoemaking and furniture industries, and at least five factories were producing ceramics for home and foreign consumption.

Most closely resembling modern factories were certain of London's porcelain, cabinetmaking and clockmaking works. The nation's largest breweries were in London, and by the 1790s there were also five large steam-powered cotton-mills. Ropeworks, foundries, and coopers' and sailmakers' workshops surrounded the port, with the naval dockyards at Deptford and Woolwich employing 2000 or more workers.

Work-related illnesses and accidents such as acid burns were common and there were few industrial regulations. Industries which needed considerable space or which involved dangerous or smelly processes were mainly south of the Thames, beyond the reach of such restrictions as did apply in the City and Westminster.

There was little or no job security for most working Londoners. Comparatively few people could rely on a single source or even type of employment to provide them with a living all year round. Seasonal work was available in the building industry and at the port, where extra labour was recruited when fleets returned from the East and West Indies and from the American colonies.

Wages remained fairly constant until the last years of the century. A labourer might earn ten shillings a week and a skilled craftsman as much as three pounds. A high percentage of workers probably belonged to Friendly Societies, a growing number of which were being established in the city. They took care of members' interests and provided financial help at times of sickness and other need.

Women's Lives

The lives led by most women in 18th-century London were determined largely by economic factors. Amongst poorer people, legal or common-law marriages survived on average for about ten years, and those women who survived childbirth and infectious diseases tended also to survive their husbands. Except in cases of comparative wealth, there was surprisingly little difference between the working lives of married and unmarried women.

Chemicals, such as those used in printing ink, were a constant hazard to the health of industrial workers.

Wife-selling was one way in which men could end an unsatisfactory marriage. Usually the wives themselves were only too happy to acquire a different partner!
GUILDHALL LIBRARY

Domestic labour of various kinds probably occupied as many as half of all London's working women, particularly before marriage. Large numbers of girls came from the provinces to meet the demand for servants, which increased with the desire of relatively less-affluent householders to have at least one maid. After marriage women often worked from home as laundresses or wet-nurses. A small but increasing number of comparatively well-educated women found employment at home as clerks and copyists for government departments.

Of those who were not working as domestic servants, just over half were involved in manufacturing work, typically as milliners or needleworkers or in the Spitalfields silk industry. Others kept shops; tax returns list female chandlers, butchers and pawnbrokers in addition to the more predictable haberdashers and lace sellers. Some widows continued to run their former husbands' businesses, although it was more usual for them either to marry his partner or senior worker and pass the business to him, or to sell up and live off the invested proceeds.

A high proportion of London's street and market traders were women. Many of them were engaged in selling fruit and vegetables, fish or other foodstuffs. Some kept pie and cookshops, whilst others sold prepared food of various kinds on the streets or were engaged in branches of the dairy trade. Seasonal work was available in the market gardens, orchards and fields surrounding the capital. This tended to attract women from the provinces, particularly Shropshire and the Welsh borders, but some London women also found work there.

Women often worked on an occasional or temporary basis, especially in times of family hardship and when seasonal work was not available for labouring men. In such cases many took to prostitution for a short time, since there was no capital outlay involved and no shortage of customers. In addition, such work was largely compatible with other commitments to home and family. Of the many thousands of women soliciting in the areas around the port and in the brothels of Covent Garden and Drury Lane, comparatively few were 'career' prostitutes.

At times of economic depression women's jobs were the first to be sacrificed. Court records paint a harrowing picture of the lives of many poorer London women at this time. There are accounts of women robbing children of their clothes, which they then sold or pawned. Even more horrifying are the stories of women forced into selling their children as 'apprentices' to thieves or as child prostitutes. Tax returns suggest that even in times of relative prosperity women earned over a third less than men, so a lone woman with dependants had a particularly difficult time. Yet women in the middle and artisan classes enjoyed an increasingly comfortable lifestyle, with servants and growing spending power.

Flat irons used by laundresses were filled with coals or charcoal so as to retain the heat necessary for ironing.

A number of shops were kept by women. William Hogarth's sisters had premises not far from St Pauls.

Shopping

Shopping as a leisure activity rather than a necessity can be traced back to the growth in consumerism which became evident in 18th-century London. Shopkeepers began to spend considerable sums of money on the interior decoration, fittings and, most importantly, the windows of their shops. The development of larger and larger bow-windowed shopfronts allowed greater space for displaying goods and for brilliant lighting to entice the public inside. As their shops became fashionable, many shopkeepers increased their social standing and became figures of fashion themselves. However, they were still inclined to follow the tradition of living on the premises with their apprentices, and to supply customers with goods made in their own workshops or produced by their own out-workers.

In the City, shops tended to be grouped according to type: mercers and drapers, for example, predominated in Cheapside, booksellers in Little Britain, and seamstresses, lace merchants and milliners in Paternoster Row. However, in the newer shopping areas such as the Strand and fashionable Bond and Oxford streets, there were shops of all kinds. Visiting London in 1786, Sophie von la Roche observed: 'Behind the great glass windows absolutely everything one can think of is neatly, attractively displayed, in such abundance of choice as almost to make one greedy'. One contemporary estimate suggests that there were around 200 different types of shop to be found in London by the end of the century.

Under such circumstances, competition necessarily became fierce. Elaborate and descriptive trade cards advertised goods and services, newspapers carried notices of special offers and a few shopkeepers even employed board-men to carry larger advertisements through the streets. The large, low-hanging, painted and gilded shopsigns that dominated the shopping streets were removed

A surviving and recently restored 18th-century shopfront in Artillery Lane, Spitalfields.

This anonymous painting of about 1730 shows a curds-and-whey seller beside the Little Conduit, with the shops of Cheapside beyond.

This engraving of a corner of the Stocks Market, where the Mansion House now stands, gives some idea of the variety of ways in which goods were sold.

by law in the 1760s. This was partly because they were considered hazardous and partly, too, because some people felt that they contributed to a lack of sophistication in the appearance of London's main thoroughfares as compared with those of Paris and other continental cities.

Opening hours were long: normally from seven or eight in the morning until eight or even ten at night. Prices in London were higher than those in the provinces and were to some extent negotiable. Amongst the first to display goods at fixed and marked prices was James Lackington at his 'Temple of the Muses' in Finsbury Square. Credit was easily obtained in such a competitive world, and pleading letters from desperate shopkeepers to their wealthy customers show that bills were often outstanding for several years! To ease everyday trading, overcome a shortage of small change (especially in the 1790s) and guard against the passing of forged coins, many shopkeepers issued their own trade tokens, which could not normally be spent elsewhere.

Hundreds of shop signs could be seen in the City before they were officially banned in the 1760s. Goldbeaters typically hung a symbolic gilded arm and hammer.

Sport and Entertainment

For most Londoners of the time there were few official holidays. These became particularly important and were celebrated with great gusto. One foreign visitor said of Lord Mayor's Day, for example, that 'at these times it is almost dangerous for an honest man, and particularly for a foreigner, if at all well dressed, to walk the streets for he runs a great risk of being insulted by the vulgar populace, which is the most cursed brood in existence'. May Day was associated with apprentices, sweeps and milkmaids, and there were bonfires on Guy Fawkes Day and Oak Apple Day, which celebrated Charles II's escape from the Parliamentarians.

May Morning, painted by John Collet in about 1760. The scene includes a chimneysweep, a hurdy-gurdy player and a milkmaid with her traditional May Morning garland or pyre of silverware.

Fairs provided other excuses for energetic merrymaking. The occasional freezing over of the Thames, as in 1739–40, gave the opportunity for holding a Frost Fair on the ice. A May Fair was held in the part of west London to which it has given its name. In the late summer the two great traditional fairs, Bartholomew Fair and Southwark Fair, attracted Londoners of all classes from nobility to beggars. Here were offered novelties and entertainments of all kinds. There were theatrical and operatic performances, exhibitions of freaks, waxworks and curiosities, as well as acrobats, musicians, quack doctors and fortune tellers, peepshows, sideshows and fairground rides.

By the 18th century there were already moves by morally outraged citizens to curb the exuberance of the major fairs. As the middle classes moved to the new suburbs south of the river, protests against Southwark Fair grew and it was finally ended in the early 1760s. Bartholomew Fair continued into the middle of the next century, when its site was taken for the new Smithfield covered market.

Fairs were not the only places where curiosities could be seen. Mrs Salmon kept a famous waxworks in Fleet Street long before Madame Tussaud arrived from Paris, and the catalogue of Don Saltero's Coffee House in Chelsea lists all kinds of amazing and even mythical 'rarities'. Those who were not drawn to such small-scale delights might have preferred the wonders of Astley's Amphitheatre near Westminster Bridge, where highly trained horses performed the most amazing feats and there were dramatic re-enactments of topical events as well as a variety of circus acts.

Londoners could escape fairly easily into the surrounding countryside, and there were still open spaces just outside the City walls. Archery was still a popular sport, as was prize fighting, which became highly organised by the end of the century. Prize fighters enjoyed aristocratic patronage and drew huge crowds and large bets. People would gamble on almost anything. Betting at cockfights, bear-baiting and dogfights was noisy and fierce, whilst over card games in fashionable salons it was a little more restrained. The love of gambling was used to advantage by the government, and state lotteries funded enterprises such as the building of Westminster Bridge.

These spurs for fighting cocks give some indication of the viciousness of the sport, which attracted people from all social classes.

Mr. Edward Harley.

Printed on the River of THAMES when Frozen over,
JANUARY 18, 1739 40.

When the Thames froze, printers took portable presses to the Frost Fairs and sold personalised souvenir prints.

The delights of Bartholomew Fair are vividly depicted in this design for a souvenir fan, dating from 1728–30.

There was also betting on the increasingly popular sport of cricket. Huge crowds went to Thomas Lord's cricket ground in Marylebone and there was betting not just on teams but on individual scores ... and also, in all likelihood, a certain amount of bribery! Cricket was also played informally in open spaces around the city, whilst bowling greens, skittle alleys and ballcourts were attached to many taverns.

Pleasure Gardens

By the late 1700s, there were over 200 pleasure gardens in and around London. Many were modelled on the great gardens at Vauxhall, Ranelagh and to a lesser extent, Marylebone. The Spring Gardens, later known as Vauxhall Gardens, were opened in 1660 on the south bank of the river, whilst Ranelagh opened in 1742 on a site on the north bank in Chelsea. The principal access to both was by water, and they offered the illusion of being in the country whilst at the same time being close to the fashionable centre.

People of many social groups went to the pleasure gardens. Some went to enjoy the musical entertainments, fireworks, masquerades and scenic and social delights. For others the gardens offered delights of a different kind, for beyond the brilliantly lit main avenues were dark corners where the social freedom of the gardens could slip easily into delicious licence! London's pleasure gardens became models for others in the provinces and on the Continent and many survived well into the 19th century.

There were also spas and 'watering places' within easy reach of the city for a Sunday afternoon outing. Sadlers Wells in Islington was particularly popular and further afield were resorts in Hampstead, Dulwich and Epsom.

The Rotunda at Ranelagh offered indoor entertainment of various kinds. The central support housed a chimney and fireplaces for use in winter.

On Sundays, too, members of the artisan and middle classes went to Hyde Park to play the game of 'see and be seen' just as their social superiors did during the rest of the week, though probably with rather more open enjoyment.

Drama and Music

Theatrical entertainments were very popular. Legal performances of spoken drama were limited, during the winter season, to the 'patent' theatres of Drury Lane and Covent Garden. Programmes at these theatres changed nightly. They began between 6 and 7 pm with a full-length play, followed by an 'after piece'. This might be anything from a farce or pantomime to a comic opera. Audiences were uninhibited in their responses, and often disruptive. Actor-managers such as Garrick and Sheridan had huge and occasionally aggressive personal followings, and there was a great deal of rivalry.

(*Above*) Silver admission tokens to Vauxhall.

(*Left*) Vauxhall Gardens, showing the Grand Walk, orchestra and supper boxes, which were decorated by such artists as William Hogarth and Francis Hayman.

'English' guitars were very popular with amateurs. A patent box fitted to the strings reduced damage to fingernails. This instrument belonged to Lady Emma Hamilton, Nelson's mistress.

David Garrick and Hannah Pritchard painted by Francis Hayman around 1747 in a scene from *The Suspicious Husband*, which enjoyed great popularity with London audiences.

Subscription tokens for the King's Theatre, Haymarket. The red one belonged to the writer Horace Walpole.

Lackington's bookshop in Finsbury Square, where 'above Half a Million Volumes are constantly on Sale'.

For wealthy subscribers, opera was available at the King's Theatre in the Haymarket. Even here violence occasionally broke out, with opera-goers disputing the relative merits of French and Italian opera and of rival performers. John Gay's *Beggar's Opera*, first performed at Lincoln's Inn Fields Theatre in 1728, marked the arrival of English opera and became enormously popular.

London was a place of great musical activity. Amateurs and semi-professionals formed clubs and societies which often met in taverns to perform instrumental and vocal music. Shrewd impresarios opened concert rooms and theatres to cater for the growing demand for subscription and benefit concerts, operas, masquerades and other musical events. The young Mozart appeared

Samuel Percy's wax model of a literary gathering at the Turk's Head tavern includes among others Dr Johnson, Sir Joshua Reynolds, Gainsborough, Charles James Fox and James Boswell.

at Hickford's Rooms in Brewer Street, and at the Hanover Square Rooms J.C. Bach and later Haydn conducted their own compositions. Handel followed George I to London and composed his operas, oratorios, ceremonial and chamber music for a number of royal and noble patrons. Among English composers, William Boyce and Thomas Arne both composed prolifically for the stage and pleasure gardens and enjoyed great popularity with London audiences.

Words and Images

Most Londoners could read, even if only at a fairly basic level, and during the 18th century the printed word grew to become a most powerful social and political force. The few newspapers established in the previous century were joined by many new ones, each copy being read many times over in the taverns and coffee houses. Periodicals such as the *Guardian*, the *Spectator* and Dr Johnson's *Rambler* contained comment and criticism on aspects of contemporary culture and society. Literary groups and clubs of all kinds were established: Steele, Addison and Swift frequented Button's in Russell Street, whilst Johnson held court at the Turk's Head in Gerrard Street.

Cheaper printing methods enabled bookseller-publishers to produce books quickly for a new reading public, drawn largely from the leisured middle classes. By 1800 there were more than twenty circulating libraries in London. The novel became a popular literary form and an increasingly effective tool of social comment, and women emerged as prolific authors. According to *The Times* in 1796, 'four hundred and seventy three novels are now in the press from young ladies of fashion.'

At the lower end of the literary market, Grub Street 'hacks' made a precarious living producing anonymous libels and satires. Their activities were complemented by those of the stationers and print sellers. Print-shop windows displayed bitingly satirical portraits and topographical prints, reflecting current political and social concerns. Prints could be bought individually for a few shillings or in series by subscription, or they could be hired in albums for the evening's entertainment, just as videos are today. Most printed images were produced by processes based on the engraving or acid etching of lines onto a metal plate, but printmakers became increasingly interested in developing tonal printing techniques, by which paintings and original drawings might be closely reproduced.

St JAMES's giving the TON.
a Soul without a Body.

} FOLLOWING the FASHION. {
Pub.d Dec.r g.th 1794. by H.Humphrey N.º 37, New Bond Street.

CHEAPSIDE aping the MODE.
a Body without a Soul.

The absurdities of current fashion were an easy target for satire and, although this print is apolitical, many such prints were published with an additional political twist.

Probably the most well-known contemporary London printmaker was William Hogarth. In 1732 he produced the first of his 'modern moral subjects', a series of engravings of 'The Harlot's Progress'. It enjoyed such popularity that several 'pirate' editions were made, resulting in Hogarth's campaigning for a Copyright Act which was passed in 1735. Recognisable London characters and places figured in his works, some of which were aimed at comparatively wealthy subscribers, whilst others were sold cheaply so that their morals might reach their intended targets. In many ways Hogarth's works are a pictorial parallel to the novels of such authors as Henry Fielding, providing invaluable insights into 18th-century London life.

Later in the century, Rowlandson and Gilray carried the by-then established tradition of pictorial satire to greater extremes of wit and even viciousness.

There is evidence of the 18th-century city to be found all over central London and the inner suburbs. The suggestions offered below are necessarily selective. Probably the most enjoyable way of exploring the 18th-century city is through reading, walking and making one's own discoveries. John Summerson's *Georgian London* (published by Penguin) provides a comprehensive list of surviving 18th-century buildings.

Spitalfields, to the north-east of Liverpool Street station, retains its strong 18th-century character. Look particularly at Elder and Fournier streets, built mainly in the 1720s. Many original facades remain in **Mayfair** and in the area around **St James's Palace**, with a few original shopfronts surviving here and there. There are virtually unspoiled early 18th-century streets tucked away immediately to the south of **Westminster Abbey** and in **Bloomsbury**.

Of the great **West End** squares, few remain unspoiled by piecemeal redevelopment, but important individual houses and occasional terraces have survived in this area. Substantial sections of the Cavendish/Harley estates remain to the north of **Oxford Street**, beyond Cavendish Square.

In spite of changing fashion, bombing and redevelopment, a number of churches survive more or less in their original form. Some idea of the variety of styles employed by 18th-century architects can be gained by visiting, for example, **Christ Church, Spitalfields** (by Hawksmoor, 1714–27), **St Mary-le-Strand** (Gibbs, 1714–17) and **St John, Smith Square** (Archer, 1713–28).

Among the more notable remaining public buildings that retain much of their original character are the **Mansion House** (George Dance the Elder, 1739–53), parts of **St Bartholomew's Hospital** (Gibbs, 1730 onwards) and of **Guy's Hospital** (1720 onwards), **Horse Guards** (to designs by Kent, begun 1750) and parts of the **Admiralty** buildings (various architects, from 1723 onwards).

Kenwood (Robert Adam, 1768) and the Italianate villa which Lord Burlington designed for his own use at **Chiswick** (1729) offer very different but equally significant examples of the kind of country retreats which wealthy people built within easy travelling and socialising distance of London.